Digging On
Dirt

by Rena Korb
illustrations by Brandon Reibeling

Content Consultant:
Paul Bloom, Ph.D. • Professor of Soil Science • University of Minnesota

visit us at www.abdopublishing.com

Published by Magic Wagon, a division of the ABDO Publishing Group, 8000 West 78th Street, Edina, Minnesota, 55439. Copyright © 2008 by Abdo Consulting Group, Inc. International copyrights reserved in all countries. All rights reserved. No part of this book may be reproduced in any form without written permission from the publisher. Looking Glass Library™ is a trademark and logo of Magic Wagon.

Printed in the United States.

Text by Rena Korb
Illustrations by Brandon Reibeling
Edited by Nadia Higgins
Interior layout and design by Ryan Haugen
Cover design by Brandon Reibeling

Library of Congress Cataloging-in-Publication Data

Korb, Rena B.
 Digging on dirt / Rena Korb ; illustrated by Brandon Reibeling.
    p. cm. — (Science rocks!)
 ISBN 978-1-60270-038-3
 1. Soils—Juvenile literature. I. Title.
 S591.3.K67 2007
 631.4—dc22
                          2007006321

Table of Contents

Dirt or Soil?

Put on your boots, go outside, and dig.
What do you find?

Did you say dirt? That's true.
But you could also say soil.
Soil is the word scientists use for dirt.

Soil All Around

Soil covers most of Earth's land.
It stretches under grass and in gardens.

Soil also lies beneath sidewalks and roads.
Sandy beaches are a kind of soil.
So are muddy riverbanks and forest floors.

Soil often reaches down about 3 feet (1 meter). But in some places the soil may be only a few inches thick.

Life-Giving Soil

Soil brings life to Earth. Plants dig their roots deep down to find water and food.

Many animals live in soil, too. Wriggling worms and burrowing groundhogs could not live without it.

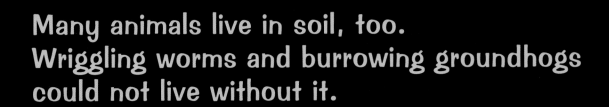

9

You couldn't live without soil.

Plants need soil to grow. Animals eat plants. Without soil, there would be no food!

Plants give off oxygen that we need to breathe. Without soil, you wouldn't be able to breathe, either!

11

Soil's Ingredients

So what are the magic ingredients in soil?

Soil is made up of rocks, air, and water. Soil is also filled with what's left of dead plants and animals after they've rotted away.

Falling leaves, twigs, and dead bugs land on the ground. As they rot, they change into rich, black humus.

Humus might not sound tasty to you, but it's like food for plants!

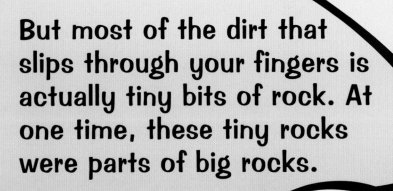

But most of the dirt that slips through your fingers is actually tiny bits of rock. At one time, these tiny rocks were parts of big rocks.

The big rocks are called parent material. That's because they are the "parents" of the small rocks that make up the soil.

How Soil Forms

Rain, snow, ice, and sunlight break the big rocks down into tiny pieces of rock.

This can take thousands of years. Then the rock pieces mix with humus to form the soil you see.

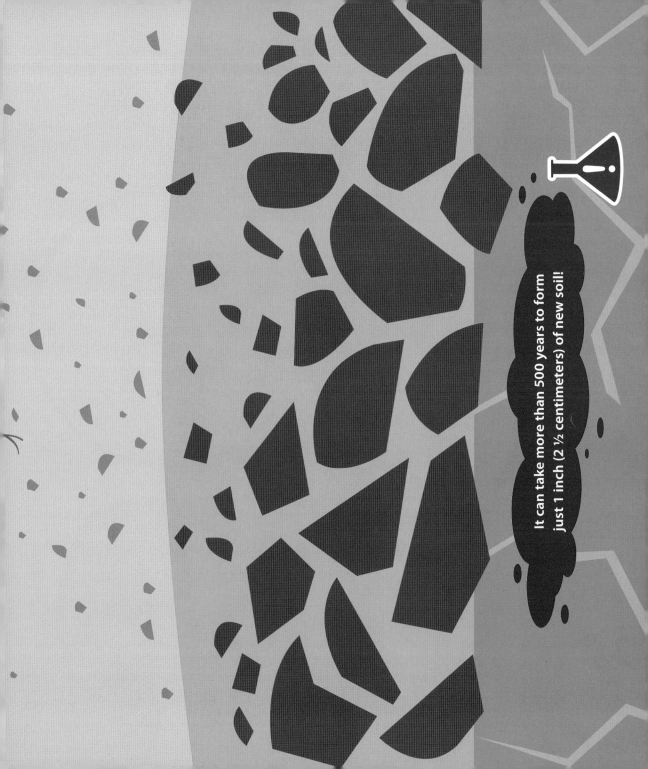

It can take more than 500 years to form just 1 inch (2 ½ centimeters) of new soil!

Sand, Silt, and Clay

Three kinds of tiny rocks make up soil. They are sand, silt, and clay.

A piece of sand is not much bigger than the head of a pin. Silt and clay are smaller still.

A grain of clay is so small, you'd need a super strong microscope to see it.

Kinds of Soil

Sandy soil is coarse and loose.
It won't hold much water.

Smooth, sticky soil has lots of clay.
When this soil dries out, it becomes as hard
as concrete. Plant roots can't grow.

On the other hand, soil with a lot of silt dries out. The soil might blow away in a cloud of dust.

Farmers try to protect soil from blowing away. They do this by covering their fields with plants and trees. Plant roots hold soil in place.

So what kind of soil is just right for growing plants? It has more sand and silt and less clay. It has the same amount of air and water. And it is rich in humus.

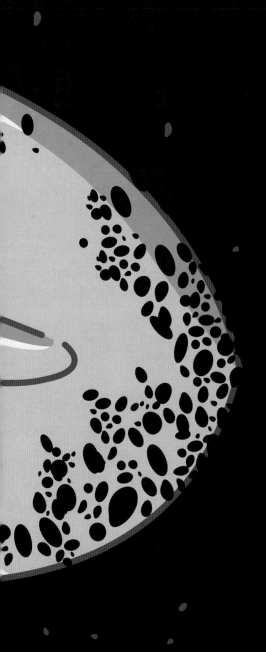

Go outside and dig again.

Is your soil dry and dusty or wet and muddy?

Do you see worms and bugs in your soil?

What is the soil like where you live?

Activity

See Soil's Ingredients

What you need:

About one cup of soil

A large, see-through jar with a lid

Water

What to do:

1. Collect the soil from outside or get it from a gardening store.

2. Put the soil in the jar.

3. Add water to the jar until it is almost full. Put the lid on tightly.

4. Shake the jar back and forth several times.

5. Wait for the soil to settle.

6. The soil will separate into layers. Bits of rotting plants might float to the top. The water underneath is cloudy from clay and some silt. The next layer from the top is silt, and sand forms the layer beneath this. The biggest rocks and pebbles fall to the bottom.

7. Try the experiment again with a different type of soil. What differences do you see?

Fun Facts

 Cotton comes from a plant, and wood comes from trees. Without soil, there would be no cotton T-shirts to wear or wood for your pencil.

 Soil can be used to build homes. Workers mix soil with water and straw. They pour the muddy mixture into molds, where it dries into bricks. The bricks can be used to build a house.

 As animals tunnel and squirm, they loosen the soil. The loose soil is good for plants. It lets their roots easily reach down.

 The tiniest creatures in soil are called microbes. You'd need a microscope to see them. Microbes help soil by breaking down dead plants and animals and turning them into humus. The more microbes there are, the richer the soil is.

 Soil comes in all kinds of colors. It can be deep red, orange, brown, or even white. The color depends on the kinds of rocks and how much humus the soil holds.

Glossary

clay—a rock particle in sand that is smaller than silt.

humus (HYOO-muhs)—brown or black matter that is made of rotted plants or animals; humus provides food for plants and helps soil hold on to water.

sand—a rock particle in soil that is bigger than silt.

silt—a rock particle in soil that is smaller than sand and larger than clay.

soil—the top layer of the earth's surface.

On the Web

To learn more about soil, visit ABDO Publishing Company on the World Wide Web at **www.abdopublishing.com**. Web sites about soil are featured on our Book Links page. These links are routinely monitored and updated to provide the most current information available.

Index